ENDEARING RHYMES FOR SPIRITUAL TIMES

WYNETTE MCKENZIE

Publisher's Note: The poems in this book are a true reflection of the poet's life experiences and emotions. All persons referenced have approved the poems and photographs concerning them.

Endearing Rhymes for Spiritual Times © by Wynette McKenzie 2014

Photographs© by Wynette McKenzie

ISBN 978-1-941726-23-5

Five Little Angels Publishing.

All photographs by Wynette McKenzie.

Copyright 2014 by Five Little Angels, LLC.

Above the Clouds

Above the cloud is where I find inner peace

A surrendering time to say the very least

It is where my burdens are rolled away

Whether in an airplane or sitting by the bay

My imagination takes me closer to heaven

Close to my Lord Jesus, breaking bread that is unleavened

Roaming in the midst of all my uncertainty

I was only trying to get a glimpse of eternity

Adultery

The Great God of all creation said thou shalt not

Commit adultery that is, even if you think you're hot

Just like taking someone's property without permission

Stealing is another law you will break with that proposition

Repent, be content and live an abundant life of joy

Flee from sin and eternal life is what you will enjoy

In a land of flowing milk and honey where you won't grow old

No money to spend and the streets are paved with gold

So abstain from sin and the lust of the flesh

Pray constantly and keep your thoughts regularly refreshed

Adversity

Philippians 3:3 says to put not thy confidence in flesh

Do not get carried away by how one may look or dress

Don't judge a book by its cover, read some pages and not read the rest

It will lead you into a cycle of never-ending mess

That will cause issues you will later be too ashamed to address

Eventually ensnared in a web of actions you will not be able to confess

Do not trust anyone with your business during a time of unrest

That person will betray you and tell your business to the press

Your friends, family and co-workers are the ones you try to impress

Thinking you had a comrade but that was the start of a disastrous test

Ponder on life's lessons and do not create a life occupied with duress

Be vigilant in creating space to be free of distractions and stress

To live a sacrificial life and honor Jesus Christ at your best

Afro

Most of my teen years I wore some kind of cool afro

You didn't know that memory still keeps me on the go

My hair is just one of the things I can rock well

It keeps me humble and makes me look so swell

Alicia

Her ambiance is quiet as the repressed ocean storms

Exhibiting a temperate spirit with creativity in all forms

Passionate as a ferocious lion weaning her young

Exists this brilliant superwoman who is so unsung

She overcomes and conquers every obstacle around her

But clinching to an authentic spiritual life is what she prefers

Unwaveringly working diligently to achieve her dreams

Praying daily to achieve them by all honest means

Alone

It's perfectly fine not wanting me around

I'm used to being quiet and not making a sound

Fear of rejection has kept me this way

If you're going to be cruel then have nothing to say

If your agenda is being unkind, that fine

I'm always here when you change your mind

God's merciful love has taught me honesty

I live by his rules since it's the best policy

Humiliate and insult me all day long

Every time you do it's only making me strong

What will it take to get a contrite heart?

Not a stone cold one that has torn us apart

Ancient Days

Are you still set in your ways?

Do those things you do bring you praise?

Remember your past cannot be erased

So just try a bit harder to erase those unhappy days

Angels

They did not have to be so sincere and hospitable to me

But they treated me like welcoming a loved one they longed to see

I was greeted with sincerity, kisses, and hugs

They knew nothing about me yet they rolled out their colored rugs

Suddenly I was in an atmosphere filled with benevolence and affection

I didn't expect anything when I felt all their warmth with no exception

It was genuine and every person was open-minded and kind

They catered to my every need while I took the time to unwind

Angelic is the expression fitting for them because of our initial greeting

Words cannot describe how friendly they were on our first meeting

I found it stress-free to be entertained by people so authentic

It was overwhelming not being treated like someone eccentric

My heartfelt thanks for their consideration of what was not planned

You are earthly angels that combined your divine wand

You'll always be cherished and bring me fond memories of your gift

The unconditional love you all gave me is enough to keep me adrift

I appreciate the world better now because of these angelic friends

I am forever thankful, but I will stop now before the tears commence

Angels in the Mist

In troubled times there will always be angels in the mist

Protecting us from perils while we continue to exist

With their gracious wings they transport us all

Ensuring us that we will never be wounded or fall

Gratitude is all we should convey to them on a daily basis

That the Almighty God sends them from His heavenly oasis

To glorify His Holy Name and safeguard us from Satan the rejected

Awaiting God's return, angels will battle until our soul is protected

Another Day

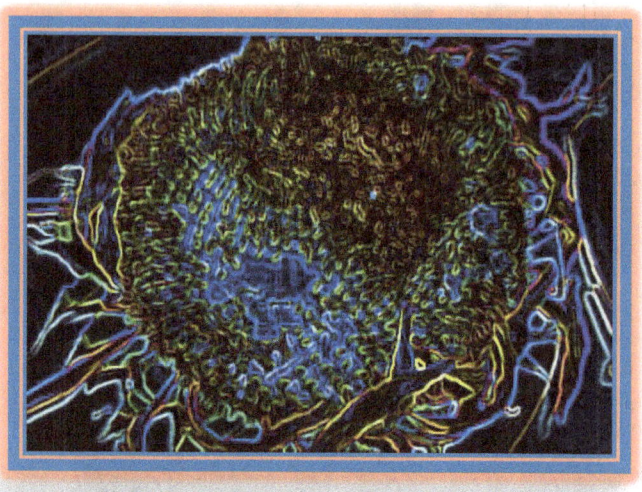

Thank you Lord Jesus for another great day

Just another day to breathe and pray

I know your day of salvation is near

Another day of confessing, surrendering, and nothing to fear

Antagonize

Do I need to ask you the question why?

Why you think it's so endearing to aggravate me until I cry

Look at your face in the mirror and ponder your own complexion

Contemplate on who you identify in the mirror's reflection

I am sure that the person or messages are not what you perceive

But you should exalt the divine communications you receive

Entertain and be on the pursuit for inner peace

Bring your burdens to the Almighty God so they can eventually cease

So until the time you decide to cast out the demons you see

Please toss them in the deep sea far away from me

Arbitrating

Do not mistake someone's compassion saying they are weak

It is better to give than to receive, just be humble and meek

If you cannot win by all means join an empathetic being

Embracing God's love which is pure and continuously seen

Try not to fault by insulting them behind closed doors

Pray for a pleasant nature doing Godly chores

Accept it as blessings and not to be mistaken for weakness

Be empathetic, pray compassionately, and fathom meekness

As Good as Gold Maybe

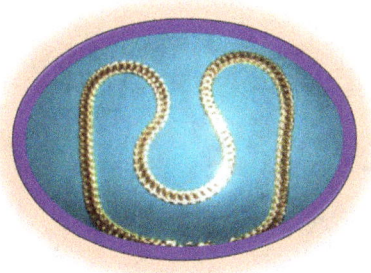

You say everything and everyone can be as good as gold

But that saying has long been foretold and appears to be growing old

You try your very best to produce gold status and don't finish first

Assuming things will not get better you do not satisfy your thirst

Some possessions can be quality silver and bronze dedications

Hold steadfast and try again for the gold in your meditations

It's okay to be second or third, your turn will come with persistence

Don't give up your dreams; persevere with every bit of your existence

Not seeing future blessings you take assets and toss them into the ocean

But when the chance arrives you'll miss your first place token

Aspirations

I will jump skip swim run and hop

I will sing shout and climb to the hill top

I will dance, teach cook garden and sew

I will laugh read and play music like a pro

I will swim, paint build and demonstrate

With God all things are possible for me to appreciate

Assurance

How amazing is God's majestic love?
Unpolluted blessings bestowed from above
Seek the Lord and you will truthfully find
It's guaranteed He will certainly not change his mind
Come to the Almighty God with great humility
It does not call for a lavish praying facility
Surrender your heart with true confessing
You'll never miss out on His marvelous blessing
His untainted word proclaims His eternal glory
Not mere listening to another man-made story
God's reward is assurance of a purpose driven life
One that is pure and not filled with constant strife
His awesome love truly is everlasting
Not like a quick fix diet or extreme fasting
His reward is the pardon of all of your sins
That is a guarantee there will always be wins
You will manifestly become His brand new creation
A person who will rise up and transform a nation

Beautiful Message Moth

A beautiful moth flew right in front of the church door in May

It jumped up and down like it had something good to say

Brother Tom and I both witnessed when it came perching down

Skipping around happily until it landed pleasantly on the ground

Brother Tom saw it from the church elevated wooded balcony

In a few seconds he came down and observed the striking moth

Equally amazed, not stopping to ask questions like how and why?

We just clutched our cameras and saw it grew even more excited

Tom's wife Connie viewed the moth encounter and was delighted

To witness all the excitement from the balcony where she preferred

It came closer, sang, then flew far away until our vision got blurred

Thank you Lord Jesus for the beautiful messages you send us each day

Ensuring us in troubled times you always remind us to watch and pray

Bernice Parker

Calmly she walks, taking short steps, simply just strutting

Wondering what she's going to do next without rebutting

Her mindset is like an enchanting epic story of affection

Like her numerous hobbies she does to perfection

Whether it is just cooking, teaching, or just a blouse to sew

Bernice uplifts your spirit and keeps you on the go

Preserve your commendable work, lovely Liberian angel

Stay humble, with that unconditional love so unchanging

Clench God's purpose fulfilled without further rearranging

Birthday

Let us celebrate, today is your birthday

On this day you will have all desires granted your way

This day the creator God Almighty molded you from the dirt

He prepared you to make a smooth touchdown on planet earth

Through the vessels of your darling mother's tender belly

Even though back then you were a little tiny and a bit smelly

Well today you blossomed and became somewhat charming

A bit more cunning than the sly fox treats that are quite disarming

So here are your lovely gifts. Not too old to delight in a splurge

Party before midnight so other festivities the next day won't merge

So blow your candles and make a cheerful aspiration

Then wish all will show up next year, because you are an inspiration

Blurred Vision

You must have had blurred vision

To think you made a moral decision

Self-righteousness and rebellion go hand-in-hand

You could have just wrestled and taken a firm stand

Instead you transported us all to the police station

Just because you couldn't process the right information

Bright Lights

Bright lights you persistently blister bright

Magnifying that radiant energy straight through the night

Inspiring graceful memories like marvelous poetry in motion

Motivating and expanding our visions beyond the deep blue ocean

Illuminating God's eternal glory like a halo for all to see

Captivating us to enter and perceive yonder in external galaxies

To get a glimpse of the joyous revelations prearranged for us

Long sighting the Father's light He gave to the world without a fuss

When it gets dim we may ponder a little and slow down

Eventually to revitalize and turn our angelic energy around

Bright lights you will glow, burn and continue to inspire everyone

To be our best until that reflection inspires us to be someone

Brighter Days

When trouble comes your way

Always know that Jesus Christ promises you a brighter day

People will envy you for the shirt off your back

Not understanding that it is wisdom they lack

Almighty God says ask and it shall be given unto you

There is no need after that promise to sit around feeling blue

Brighter days are around the corner and that is true

Broken Heart

How can anyone mend a broken heart?

Is there special needle and fabric to sew it and not tear it apart?

Can a doctor prescribe a special medication?

Will it be stabilized without putting it in sedation?

Can a chef cook a specific dish that may be of any appeal?

Will a scientist muster up an experiment that will make it to heal?

Can a preacher preach a good sermon that would be nourishing?

Will sewing, cooking, experimenting or preaching be flourishing?

Can it be sufficient to restore a broken heart?

To bring it back to before it was torn apart?

Bubbles

I see hundreds of bubbles floating in the water while popping

Some big and small ones ascended to the sky then kept dropping

It was quite fascinating to see how some just kept rising up higher

While others observed were dressed by the sun's glaze in rainbow attire

Eventually they all just disappeared as they just kept popping

Caught

The sneaky lovers just got caught

Scorned and disgraced is not what they had sought

Even though it took them several years

Reaping what they sow is among their foremost fears

It is quite testing to cross another man's junction

Contemplating on it is enough to barely function

The two thought they played a fair game

What did they gain? Please! Even pit bulls can be tamed

If the grass was so much greener on the other side

Why are there so many scandalous things they try to hide?

Character

It is mainly your actions

That cause strong reactions

Your atmosphere should show signs of simplicity

Instead it's overwhelmed with complexity

Try to tone it down and make it notable

Easily accessible and portable

When your personality cultivates into being nice

It will become as sweet-smelling as spice

Cheers For the Game

Everyone get ready to cheer for the game

Jumping up and down like we are all insane

Pom-poms, whistles, caps, and Nike gear

Marching on like we just don't care

Home team wishes and opponents dream

Pizzas, sodas, music band, and flavored ice cream

Hotdogs, hamburgers, Gatorade, and chips

Cheerleaders, families, vendors, and coach's tips

Players angry at referee's dishonest call

Just come enjoy the game and have a ball

Paramedics, police officers, bruises and fall

It's all worth it when the winner takes all

Childish

Call me a memory hoarder

I'd rather be that than an aircraft boarder

Not because I hate flying

It's just that with these possessions, I have stopped buying

They are whimsical, charming and full of character

Come and see me at play, like I am the contractor

By now, you would like to know

What keeps me vibrant and on the go

It makes me cherish my childhood days

It has fashioned my character in many ways

What do you think is giving me all those joys?

Not anything but my favorite childhood toys

Church Families

Church families gives us the balance we desire

They uplift us spiritually and keep us inspired

Everyone shares an extraordinary collective role

To love the Lord the Jesus Christ as their main goal

Every person keep doing your best to make it to paradise

In the meantime remember this good advice

That Lord Jesus has already sacrificed and paid the price

Cold Breeze

Cold breeze can provide me great comfort and ease

Other times it just makes me sneeze

On several occasions it soothes and closes my pores

But to me cold breeze feels best bundled up and strolling outdoors

Criticize

Before you condemn someone try to walk a mile in their shoes

See the world from their perspective before you even have a clue

Be compassionate and always lend them a helping hand

We are more alike than we are different that you will understand

We just process things at unrelated times and at a different pace

But that is the beauty of God's creation that makes up the human race

Cry

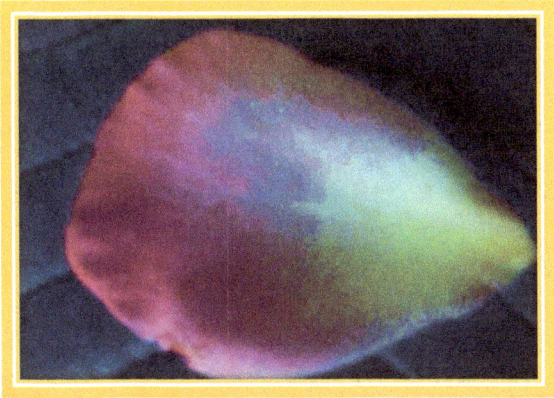

It is quite okay to have a good cry

Let the teardrops fall and do not query why

It will be therapeutic at best

Your joys and troubles will get a rest

You'll forget about your predicaments all the while

And absorb that the healing was worth the cry

Daddy's Doubles

Daddy please can I have a candy? Sure, can I have one too?

Every request came in doubles and only enough to make him blue

I desire the left, no you take the right, and this is enough for now

I am hungry, I need to get in my corner and hide for good a chow

Will it be Barney or Sesame Street? There is no need to have a big fight

You will never win with dad and by no means will you ever be right

Daddy, Daddy please informs us, who do you love the most?

Please! Double trouble, enough. Sit down, be quiet and eat your toast.

Dear Abuser

How long will you cause others riveting pain?

What will it take for you to become justly sane?

Why not straighten up and fly right, forgive and forget

Before you do something that you will truly regret

How would you feel if this was done to your daughter?

Will she be stable or will she become a mockery for laughter

Think about a positive legacy that will mold your life on this earth

Start with thanking God and the mother that gave you birth

Then surrender and confess your sins to The Lord Jesus Christ

Pray for forgiveness and know that your life came with a price

Dear Almighty God

Dear Almighty God will you open the windows of heaven and let me in

I am desperately trying to cope with this world of abundant sin

Your begotten Son Christ Jesus taught me to exercise endurance

To make my faith joyful and have more assurance

However everyday temptation and sin abound

The wicked one is constantly trying to make his rounds

Can I just visit you on a short vacation?

I know you love me and that I need no indication

I just long to see you but know I have to surely wait

In the meantime I will continue to build on my growing faith

Devotion

No more accusing, misusing or abusing

Just try to be kind, gentle and affectionate

Then devotion is what you will appreciate

Smile, be positive and exuberant

Live a meaningful life and stay jubilant

Disconnect

She approached, declared, and she wept, yes she certainly wept

We saw the emotions in her eyes, all the grief and dismay she long kept

All she wanted was our attention and unconditional affection

We eventually figured out that she felt nothing but rejection

We were so oblivious to her appeal for our assistance

We just watched her enveloped in despondency with little resistance

A perfect world of glowing archangels is what she had envisioned

But our disconnect with her cries needed some serious revision

Were the tears, wounds, grief and emotions enough for us to connect?

Or do we have to wait for death to realize we disconnect?

Divine

From the beginning to the end He will always be there

He will always love you, even if you really don't care

He will give you strength and honor, just listen to His story

So you can be like Him and inherit eternal glory

Call on Him always and remember His name

I am The Alpha and The Omega Lord Jesus proclaims

Doodles

All we did this semester was fill our papers with doodles

My classmate and I, resembling two little poodles

We just nodded and fantasized about sleeping

When the professor lectured we felt like weeping

We carefully examined all of our classmates

Established that we were equally bored at alarming rates

Watching the clock and waiting to gallop through the gates

Education

Trying to stay focused on education

Requires devotion and self-determination

Ignoring snares that will lead you to fail

Is definitely for the resilient and not the frail

Keep on keeping on and never give up

Finish the race and reach the mountain top

Emilee

Emilee is as beautiful as a tulip flower

Delightful to be around every ticking hour

Loves to explore every detail of toys on the floor

Just waiting to venture out when someone opens up the door

She adores her charming caregiver Susie of course

Who's her strength and parents' true driving force

Curious Emilee will travel the world one day

But France will always be her favorite place to stay

She has already travelled there before

Maybe one day she'll take Susie on a grand tour

Emotions

Please leave me unaccompanied so I can just cry

Alright try hard to tickle me so my tears can dry

That bad memory is making me hide in the closet and sigh

Miriam just cheered me up and gave me Oreo cookies that were fried

That A+ I got last semester was so exciting that I kissed the B goodbye

Will I be in school forever? To my amazement it is worth a try

Who will love me if I drop out; I know God loves me all the while

Crying, sighing and smiling, my emotions will change by and by

Endure

Only our Heavenly Father keeps us unremittingly strong

Picks us up when we fall and when things collapse and go wrong

He whispers softly and tenderly in our ear

Reminding us that He is always there

With that promise there is nothing or no one to fear

So hang in there, with His comfort in time you will heal and repair

Energy

Sometimes we get the green light that keeps us vibrant

Only to encounter a red light that reduces our speed

Then the amber light blinks and confuses our moves

Other times we never wait for a signal, we just go with the flow

Everlasting Love

I would like to have an everlasting love

One that is always blessed from the Almighty God above

If you are trying to fathom my love think of it as an ecstasy pill

Us spending time together climbing and rolling down the hill

Like a cellphone contract it will continue to rollover

And wrap around you like a four leaf clover

Every Inch of You

Every inch of you is measured with care

From the tip of your toes to your unique hair

Like wandering alone in the remote forestry

Is that where I think of you and write lines of poetry?

It is amazing if those thoughts would continue to grow

I must halt and contemplate, or they may just continue to flow

Exercise

Whether on a bike, lifting weights, running or walking

Put aside the excuses and let your body do all the talking

Exercise to be healthy is the ultimate goal

Before your bones get rigid and deterioration takes it's toll

Find a friend or buddy, or go alone starting as a small project

Lifelong habits will have a boundless effect

Whether hourly, daily or weekly, get the body moving

The end results will unquestionably keep you grooving

Like everything else do it in moderation

Just a thought for your consideration

Father

From the beginning of the embryo

You left your child's life and said you had to go

Why didn't you just step up to the plate?

Tried harder and just have a little more faith

Every house certainly has an owner

Just be a father and not a sperm donor

It is not all about having a fancy car

Just stop to think what you've accomplished so far

You still have time, it is not too late

Quit avoiding the issue and making it a great debate

Fearless

From the time I was aware of fear I decided to be fearless

Fearless doing the things I dare myself without being careless

Careless but assuring if anyone harmed me, they'd make me tougher

Toughness yields ethos that will aid me when times get rougher

Rougher time's survival will strengthen me to endure

Endurance will remind me to fear zilch but the Almighty God above

Heaven is where I'm bound fearlessly and will ascend like mighty dove

Fish

I try to be like a blue fish textured and tough

Trying hard not to crumble when times get rough

Hanging on to my dignity, not showing my whiskers like the catfish

There are times when the sight of the pink salmon stimulates my senses

Motivating me not to be like a tilapia, thinking things are too complex

Still I'll fight like the sword fish with my weapon to the bitter end

Five Little Angels

Five little angels entered my existence

Crawling, bawling, and growing with no resistance

At a time most needed, to escape much friction

They taught me to love with a strong conviction

Right before I almost went insane

It was far better than seeking dishonest fame

Words cannot describe the joy they brought

I never regretted it or wasted a thought

The happiness and surprises they give me everyday

Makes me forget the pain I was in anyway

Birthdays, vacations, you never know, I will just continue to pray

Besides my Lord Jesus, these angels keep me on the go

Flexibility

I would like to have some flexibility

To have enough time and ability

To accomplish all my goals and visions

Without the burden of making a bad decision

Having the mindset to start and finish every task

Setting an example so not one person dare ask

If my conviction is in proportion with the vision I see

Or will I have ample devotion and flexibility

Focus

I do not care for an exquisite vacation

Or moving to any prime location

My only desire is to acquire a good education

So I can teach a yearning nation

What my teachers prudently taught me

Just how to be the next big sensation

To pass it on to the next generation

Maybe then they can also proclaim

That it was worth the sacrifice to gain liberation

The one God gave us after His Divine creation

Only then can I say that I truly lived up to my own expectation

Forbidden Fruit

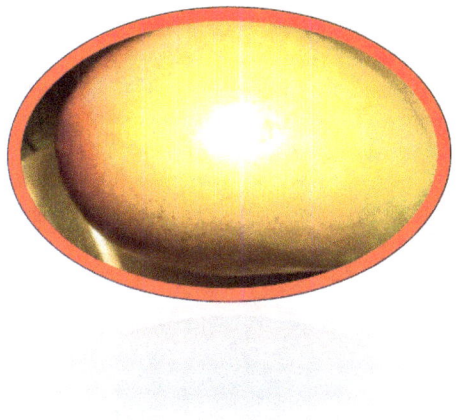

If forbidden fruit is supposed to be such a sweet fit

Why is it you have to hide to get a bite out of it?

Prohibited from the exquisite seeds to the drenched extract

That is what bewildered Eve to eat from the tree of life to be exact

So much discomfort and nothing to really gain

Leave the forbidden fruit or you might just drive yourself insane

Gems

Rare gems are hard to find

Precious jewels that are generous and very kind

Preaching the Gospel of Christ Jesus in and out of season

Reminding everyone that salvation in Christ is their only reason

Get It

Just in case you did not hear

I adamantly made it very clear

I am not about to put my life back in confusion

That is the devil's world of chaotic delusion

Hope you get it then, now, always and forever

The moral of this story is get it now or never

Gifts

Everyone has at least one of them

Practice them or share it with a friend

Utilize them when you are driven

They are strictly and purely God-given

Gifts can take you to a comfortable place

Where you can make a difference in the human race

God

God is so merciful, kind and good all the time

He created the whole universe for us just fine

We are just enjoying it, without it costing us a dime

Persevere until the end and with him we will all dine

Sharing in His glory, he prepared for us like fine wine

Never give up, smile a while, and just keep smiling all the time

God-Fearing

The fear of the Lord is the beginning of knowledge

It is a far cry from graduating from college

Fearing God has nothing to do with how book smart you are

When you fear the Lord you are His shining star

Good Old Days

So much for the good old days

When I was not so set in my ways

Mom made me feel free, that to me was very appealing

As long as I did not act on anything I was feeling

Now children, it is the same thing I have to pass on

So as long as I am around I will sing you this song

Good People

Good people make the world go around

Other people make the atmosphere go down

Which one will you elect to be?

To leave a true legacy and learn to be free

Hand-in-Hand

If we stay hand in hand

Maybe then we will fully understand

That the world was not centered on all our plans

Nor did we enter to give others foolish demands

We just need to bond together and not compromise

Just support, embrace, cultivate and learn to be wise

Happiness

Happiness is putting God Almighty first in everything you do

Acknowledging that He sent His only Begotten to die just for you

It is being cheerful and free to be exactly what God created you to be

Caring for the less fortunate and constructing life as pleasant as you see

Being humble, submissive, and putting the interest of others foremost

Happiness conveys happiness; it sparkles through you to the utmost

Happiness is loving freely and winning total affection in return

It is the joy of benevolent and receiving what you arrange for and earn

Patience and contentment is a plus, do not be hasty for anything

Your perseverance will produce happiness and that truly is something

Herb Teas

I love drinking all flavors of herb teas

Sipping them gives me a feeling of tranquility

Chamomile calms my nerves and gives me less anxiety

To fashion me to be a more productive person in society

Cranberries help me avoid infections

I usually stay afloat and have better connections

Green tea helps my heart feel at ease

I drink it early when I'm enjoying the beautiful morning breeze

My favorite one has to be the sweet and delicious mango

It keeps me dancing and performing the tango

Hold Me Tight

Hold and squeeze me very tight

Please transport me to a different height

Position your hand and take hold of my hand

Raise my pressure to the next level where the sensation is grand

Until I release my loneliness and desire

Only then my sweltering heart will put out the fire

Homework

I did not cry because of what you had to say

I knew exactly what you were trying to convey

The homework was becoming quite a chore

Time consuming and quickly a bore

I am trying to highlight on it a bit

Only to discover my tiresome effort just did not fit

Constructive criticism surely heals the soul

It brings you closer to your one real goal

Find a theme that fits the assignment just right

Eventually the homework will be complete and out of your sight

Hope

Only when we die there is no hope

So cheer up and leave no period to mope

Quit the excuses and just appreciate being around

Contemplate quietly and cultivate without a sound

Dream big and don't let opportunities miss you

Think positive and do not wait for your demise

Make the best of everything and let it be concise

Hypocrite

Try not to live your life as a hypocrite

But attempt to be truthful and make an effort to admit

We all sin and fall short of God's marvelous glory

Remember not to build iniquity because it generates a great story

Think of the true purpose of your existence

Free yourself from the temptation of sinning

So you can set a good example and focus on soul winning

I Gravitate

I gravitate towards the love of Almighty God The Most High

I gravitate towards His unconditional love that I can never deny

I gravitate to my Savior Jesus Christ God sent to die for my sins

I gravitate towards the Holy Spirit that provides me millions of grins

I gravitate towards unselfishness and positive behavior

I gravitate towards kindness and the love of Jesus Christ my Savior

I gravitate towards honesty and being safe and secure

I gravitate towards salvation and a relationship with God that's pure

I gravitate towards peacefulness and unity

My gravitation is compelled by my devotion to the Lord in the Trinity

I Love You

I love you immensely when you are up

I love you tenderly when you are down

I love you when you are quiet and not making a sound

I love you when you are flamboyant and gaudily unbound

I Wish To

Be blameless and upright like Job

Have dreams like Daniel

Taken to heaven like Enoch

Be a prophetess like Moses's sister Miriam

Converse with God like Moses

Be a beautiful queen like Esther

Be faithful and fearless like Abraham

Be as brave as Isaac

So much for my imaginary wishes

They are endless like a sea full of millions of fish

If I do not appreciate me the evil one will get in the midst

I will continue to be the best I can be

My creator God Almighty has made me this way

And this is how He expects me to stay

Incomplete

Trying to survive all the unhappy news

Is just giving me the summertime blues

I am still observing and searching for clues

Of why I had been so abused

Right now I must confess

That I was truly just a hot mess

I am no longer trying to wear that revealing dress

Neither will I continue dressing to impress

I am now mending that enormous hole

That took such an emotional toll

Spiritual recovery is my main goal

To be supported and try to heal my tired soul

So try to embrace me and be very kind

Only then can I heal my fragmented mind

By letting all my burdens unwind

Peace and happiness I will eventually find

Indifference

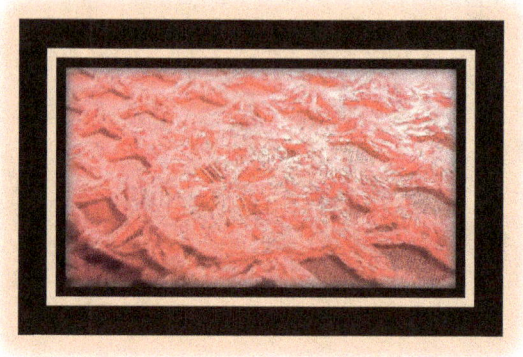

When I stayed away from you

I did not mean to make you blue

Something you did caused me to stumble

That triggered our relationship to crumble

It does not mean that you are unstable

I will resume our friendship when I am truthfully able

Right now it is on the mend

I know that is hard for you to comprehend

So as for now only time will tell

If in the end it will all be well

Infants and Toddlers

These little angels need lots of love and respect

Unconditional devotion is all they expect

Give them all the freedom to imitate

Uninterrupted play is what they really appreciate

Their environment must always be safe for them to play

Just monitor them so they will not crawl or run away

Stimulate their minds and imagination with picture books and toys

These will bring the greatest rewards and abundant joys

Jake

Jake is like a huggable little teddy bear

Up and down he bounces in his fancy gear

Looking for new things in the room to discover

Like a scientist locating things to uncover

While his charm is just a bit beguiling

I love the way he just glares and keeps on smiling

It's intriguing to see how he cuddles his toys

Definitely was a delight to share all of his joys

He is just a dream to his family, especially mom and dad

I was blessed to observe him and was quite glad

To witness him in a few weeks crawling and sitting up

In just a few more months he'll be drinking from a cup

Jeopardy

It took years for you to contemplate

Just how to scheme and eat from our family plate

After your exploitation stunt of work, sport and friendship

Your undisclosed conversations just slipped

You eventually ran out of fruitless steam

The words trustworthiness and longevity was triggering you to scream

To steal time creating for yourself memories of someone else's life

Just because your life was unpleasant, confused and full of strife

Like most life lessons, it could have been a blessing in disguise

For you to wake up, motivate yourself and learn to be wise

Jokes

Come and listen to my silly jokes

From little children to grown up folks

Laughter is good for the belly

Like sweet honeycomb and guava jelly

July Heat

Everything around me seems quite scattered

My memories are becoming foggy and shattered

The heat's got me in a world of confusion

If I was not sane I would be in a state of delusion

The air conditioner is busted, the fan is no better

So hot that I may have to send God a pardon letter

To save me from scratching and tearing my back

Also ease my need for liquids that's triggering a panic attack

So I chased the winter blues away but I must wait for fall

Loving all seasons and recognizing that they will finish after all

Just in Case

Just in case you become very sad

It was not my intention to make you so mad

So smirk, lighten up and just be glad

If indeed you are still annoyed with me

Forgive me, alleviate the wrath and you will see

It is just the flip side of my love

And the essence of it thereof

Kindness

When you show kindness with true love and devotion

You will experience gratitude with wholesome emotion

Kindness given should not be equal to the acts of kindness received

It is always a heartfelt gift that is exceedingly perceived

Last Night

I dreamt about beautiful humming birds

Singing enchanting melodies in my ears in low cords

What they were trying to sing I do not know

They continued their tunes approaching five in a row

One captured my attention with a very high note

Letting me know I am here for you and not to provoke

When I woke up my day was filled with inner peace

These cupid hummingbirds desired for me to know

That God is love and will be there every second as I grow

Let Me Be

Let me be me

And you just keep being you

Only then you will eventually see

That we are different and that is the truth

Lillian

Hello angelic little Lillian

You are so fragrant and one in a trillion

Oh wait, I just want to change my mind

Remarkably so adorable, you are one of a kind

I love to hear all yours sounds of animals on a farm

That is why your mom and dad think you are a charm

I can't say how much I will miss you

Just to think of it is making me blue

Looking For Me

I was looking profoundly for me

Desperately looking for inklings of who I wanted to be

Intently looking at what I had become

I walked down the stairs quietly one by one

I then heard a voice saying think about this, have a little meditation

But let me assure you that I created you without any hesitation

What you think you are to others really does not matter

That is only a source of a lot of chatter

What really matters is that nobody can be you

You are created for a reason and that much is true

To be accepted for every season

No need to keep looking for you and trying to find a reason

You are here at this time and you need no clue

You were bought with the blood of Christ, no need to ever be blue

Love

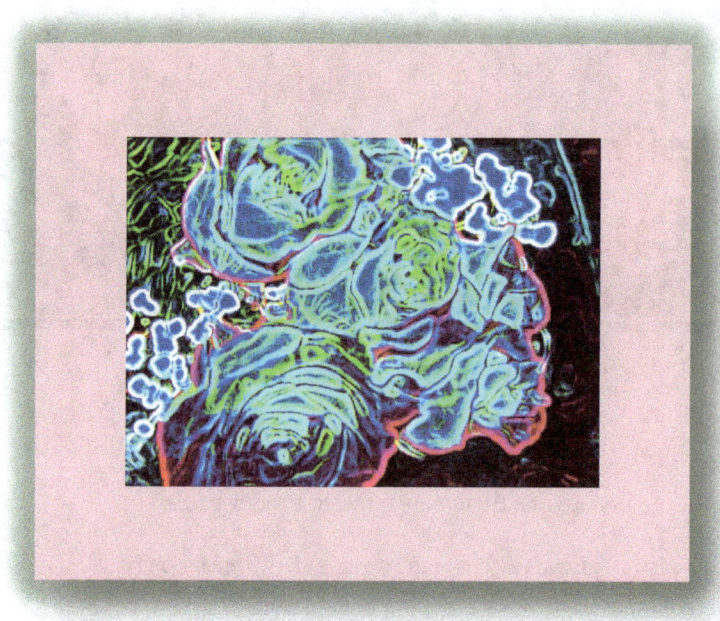

They say love is sweet like sugar cane

That is only if the parties involved elect to remain sane

They say love must be patient and always kind

That depends on if it's mutual and no one changes their mind

Lust

An enchanting escape to romantic Paris

Led me in the arms of charming Mr. Faris

Lights, camera, action and couture fashion

Bewildered me to a sizzling night of passion

With future promises of an everlasting love

It was clear this was not a counsel from above

Left with a fragmented heart and inner screams

Undoubtedly these thoughts were just a lustful dream

Mama and Baby Me

Mama bore me in a world of unconditional love

Quite fragile seeking and looking innocent as a dove

Soon I had to transition to being authentic and grown

Bearing my burdens and reaping what I have sown

Only God knows my beginning and end

I will try to continue living as a blessing he had send

Thriving for genuineness and really trying to comprehend

Once there is life there will continue to be much hope

Living it to the fullest and not taking it as a mere joke

Marriage

Inquisitive and foolishly in love, I decided to tie the knot

Promise of love to the end; I tried not to think I was put on the spot

Blissful days, irrational ways, serious love making till the break of day

Strong declarations wondering how to make this adoration stay

Wham, whap, wee came precious babies, not forgetting the one I lost

Pleasurable nurturing them, no regrets or trying to calculate the cost

Had to digest the bad news, my last child was miscarried in a bathroom

Never thought the loss of my last pregnancy would make me feel doom

Can't turn back the hands of time, so I chose the fragmented parts

One day I hope to build my gems a home that is state of the arts

Back to marriage: it started with me, myself, and I then lighten up

The moment after lightening up it was just him, enough to fill my cup

I'm trying to make it sound like six of us, but it is just two, no more

Two individuals; not three or four, everyone else needs trot out the door

Obstacles may come, along with countless ups and numerous downs

But marriage is God sent to be cherished until you're no longer around

Mary Kay Ash

A beautiful, smart, and driven woman at work and play

Taught women to look their best and glow like the sun's ray

All I can say is once you use anything Mary Kay

You feel transformed like there is no other way,

You're a new person, so her products are here to stay

There is no comparison, that is final and that is all I have to say

Placing God first is how she should be portrayed

Math Tutor

Can I please be ensured a math tutor?

Perchance I won't take this pain out on my new scooter

Undertaking any math class is far too scary

Frankly it's making my eyes much too teary

Dear God please make this to some extent imaginary

Like being the owner of my own math library

Okay maybe not, that is quite on the contrary

Just a lovely vacation on an island where it is bright and airy

Me and Mini Me

When you entered my life you truly gave it a new meaning

It was a long drought before you came out and started screaming

By then I was dreaming of a boy, what a teacup full of wishes

The blissful jiffies approached and I'm sure I gave you a million kisses

My mini and I have a mutual respect for each other in our hearts

God sent with an unconditional love, till death do us part

Me Myself and I

I am going here

I bought this for myself

Going to buy something for me

I planned a trip for me

I did this for myself by myself

Hello, God first then the three of you

ENOUGH ALREADY!

Memories

Some memories make us smile

Some make us cry for a while

Some make us jovial and some make us sad

Some make us contemplate about things we wish we had

But memories are cherished and keeps us prepared

To uncover our memory box we are eager to share

Mental Wreck

I was once a mental wreck

Soon I had to get a reality check

Trying hard to please everybody

Not acknowledging that I was somebody

An unblemished reality is what I could not see

That if I was going to build my strength it was all up to me

Michael Jackson

When I heard the unhappy news

That was the beginning of some serious blues

I prayed for the Almighty God to resurrect him

But this time I just did not win

I know his songs' energy and goodwill

Will continue to give me great pleasure

Like my childhood toys that I keep and treasure

The grief is unceasing depending on the days

However that anguish has changed some of my ways

Call me irrational and I will reply

I was one of his biggest fans and that is no lie

Michael S. Glasser

Patient, down to earth, quiet, and relatively profound

No need to become nervous whenever he is around

He humbly greets you with the utmost respect

Displays grace in his work that enables us to connect

A persona that unites us to the world of poetry and art

His reflections and insightful teaching is what sets him apart

Miriam

Watching the transformation of your athletic passion

Is an unspoken determination in a steady fashion

A charisma that has developed through positive expression

Fortitude and productive liberation from economic repression

With humility and encouragement you will continually succeed

Your complete adoration and goodwill will surely proceed

Focus on your personal development with exceptional respect

Formulate a pattern of growth that nobody can reject

Do not have reservations about anyone's insignificant predictions

Develop a strategic advantage without any contradictions

Missing You

Since your death, I am not sure how I can continue to function

My last memory is when your body was driven by your junction

Holding my fast thumping heart that was heavy and quite weary

Wiping my weeping eyes like a slow dripping faucet red and teary

These lonesome days without your presence is taking its toll

I plead with the angels to keep me sane and stay on patrol

To mend slowly the fragments of my lonesome heart

That could only be restored if we were never apart

For now comfort and pleasant memories is all I hope to find

Clutch on to positive ones and let all sorrows unwind

Mom

If I am going to emphasize

Without any dreary compromise

Mom you have always been fair

Scrutinizing every single detail

You may not have always been there

But I know that from afar you always cared

For everyone, you made boundless sacrifices

Fighting and protecting with all devices

There were times when you had to grin and bear

Nevertheless you survived eluding every tear

Truly you are the family's unwavering rock

You continue fighting for everyone to stay on top

Mom Separated From Her Dear Child

Who takes a child away from their beloved mother?

The divine vessel of their precious existence, Oh brother

Who separates that child from their mom's umbilical cord?

Using a mom in the name of love and happiness, My Dear Lord!

Exhausting the melodramatic line, I will love you until death do us part

Stealing the child right out of the comfort of mom's tender heart

Your only alibi was to get your lawyers to call her crazy and insane

Splitting the child from the mom that carried her for your own gain

Where are the words respect, and devotion for a human's life?

Was this not the same woman you climaxed with, and made your wife?

How do you sleep at night? Will heaven's gate accept your indignity?

Or will you repent Dad and face reality

Shame on you and your lawyers that muster up such deception

You played the role of murder they wrote well, no exception

She is lifeless while you live; she cannot even visit her precious child

Jesus is coming soon, please don't wait til it's too late to run and hide

Musical Alarm Clock

Wow, it abruptly came time to be up and finish my dream

Instead I reacted and then made a very loud scream

I know my alarm clock aided a purpose for a little while

But just a few more minutes would have made me smile

I was just trying to remember my wonderful dream

See I was about to become the owner of a football team

Oh please, what was I even thinking?

The contract vanished as soon as my eyes started blinking

I did not have the things my heart aspired

Or even journeyed to the places my wistful soul desired

I knew the clock was doing the job with decency

It sure strained to unburden all that complacency

However the moral of this tick tock dreamy story

Was for me to think of Christ Jesus' eternal glory

Salvation is near and the door will soon be padlocked

Then there will be no need for my musical alarm clock

My Brothers and Sisters

My brothers and sisters are not just pieces of me

It is not just DNA, look closer and you will see

That we love and share lots of common goals

We try to stick to and identify with our own humble roles

My brothers and sisters are a blessed gift from the Creator

With my siblings in my life, I do not need a negotiator

To me they are a representation of love and appreciation

Producing a reminder of God's beautiful creation

They give me strength in all my social dealings

Unconditional love for my siblings are my true feelings

My Guardian Angel

Some people need a lot of comfort

Some are looking for emotional support

Some may be seeking gratifying pleasure

Some try to hide their true feelings

While others try to defend them

But you carried me to a place

Where all was prayed away with grace

You comforted me when I was unhappy

You cheered me up when I was annoyed

You made sure no one disrespected me

You are kind and patient even when it is impossible

You are committed to a true spiritual life

With an unconditional love for everyone else

You are a light in everyone's life that shines so bright

That is why you are my guardian angel Luritz Parker

My Hands

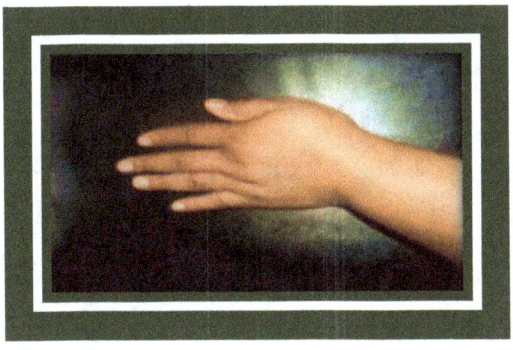

This is a picture of my actual hand

I gaze at it and try hard to understand

That what I do with it next will soon show

I use it to pray, cook, clean, help others, and sew

What will it do afterward I do not know

Whatever it does it will keep helping me grow

And with conviction leave my heart with an after glow

My Love

There is obviously nobody that makes me feel the way you do

Not a soul that can comprehend my feelings even when I am blue

To me you can understandably do nothing wrong

That is why our love is ever so strong

Infatuations may originate and they may go

But it will take a resilient woman to love you from head to toe

My love for you can only withstand the test of time

Almighty God has made us one and you will always be mine

My Organs Shattered

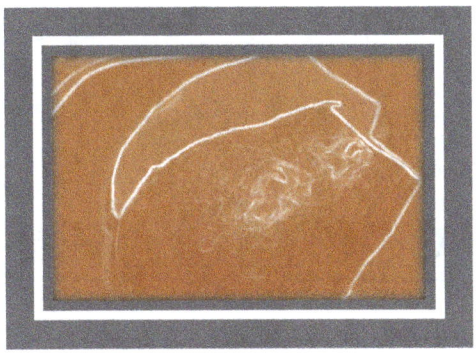

To the ground my internal organs fell then got shattered

With your every move and gesture they were all scattered

My heart crumbled by your sudden callous look

My kidneys refused to function then folded like a hook

When you turned and ignored me my heart ceased pumping

Only to make it weak, skip a beat, and start jumping

That did not go very well with my lungs

Oxygen slowly cut off leaving a dry feeling on my tongue

My muscles became painful and filled with tension

When you refused to concede or give me any attention

Suddenly a sharp pain targeted my spleen

It left me in disbelief wondering how you turned so mean

Until you decide to transform and turn things around

Then I can get my shattered organs off the ground

My Stepdad

You left America and your family, flying over mountains and seas

You did not count the cost, expenses or challenge the outrageous fees

Landing in Guyana—a land of exotic parrots, toucans and monkeys

Trying a new culture, settling, and giving yourself a slight ease

Next came a culture shock, while you were enjoying the ocean breeze

Thrills of a foreign land came with all its things that appease

Like broken marriages, separations and starting a new life overseas

Inheriting a ready-made family was a highlight and your honorees

You catered to our needs never showing signs of being displeased

You introduced us to new music while you enjoyed rice and peas

We showed off our calypso and reggae while wining down to our knees

You traded apples for guavas, five-finger, papaw and more please!

You trained us to be our best in weather that hit 100 degrees

Brought us to America in December where we faced a winter freeze

We traded sapodillas for melons and seaweed from under seas

Now you are happy we're alive and well, you're now a tranquil retiree

You lived a life of dignity and that is where we all agree

Thanks for opening us to a world of two cultures with all your expertise

Nivea

There is not enough words to say about Nivea

She is as sweet as the honey down in Bolivia

Such a loving and vibrant little soul

That loves to give herself a pink mole

On her face of course, trying to stand on her toes

She takes her imagination where her new adventure goes

Like biting wood from the corners of the center

Where she gets optimistic ideas her mind can enter

She will soon be a great leader that rules a nation

Inspired to build studios with their own pedicure station

In the meantime she'll bite on her wood chips

While the teacher sings and she moves her hips

Nothing Makes Sense Anymore

We were created by the one and only God of all creation
We soon forget and abort babies formed to build this nation
We fly first class on the same plane that coach flyers are on
We fail to realize that if the plane crashes, we're all gone
We send an innocent person to jail to cover up our offenses
But when we are guilty we muster up all kinds of defenses
We try to market products with the fanciest sales pitch
When the initial price is enough to leave us in a ditch
We abandon loved ones thinking the grass will be greener
Only to discover the outcome was meaner
We build mansions just to get in one bed to sleep
When the bills arrive we go into a corner and weep
We attend concerts to watch someone perform their story
Rather than devote to the coming of Christ in His glory
We try to experiment on people for foolish gain
When the needy cry for help we neglect to hear their pain
We preach about things that we expect others to follow
Yet we do not practice what we teach, which is so hollow
The opulent boast about wealth and belittle the lowly
Not realizing their empire will crumble surely but slowly
So why not try to be humble, patient, and kind
Your life will be far greater than you will find

Oldies but Goodies

It is time to completely play the dupe

Turn up the stereo and crank the oldies

Dash to the trunk, turn the key and grab the halter top

The platform shoes could be a good mix to the fit

Okay crank up the oldies, but do not drink just reminisce

Happy memories will assist you through the rough ones

So listen to the oldies and do not contemplate back too far

Just enough to brush off the sad feelings and add golden thoughts

Okay that is enough, remember it was good to cheer up and get by

Prayers are the best substitute, just saying some oldies help too

Overtime

I once worked 200 hours overtime

Quite tedious but I always wanted to try it sometime

The feedback I got was very undesirable and low

Someone asked me if I just had some hot sex, which was a blow

Yet another asked if I was consuming pills

How discourteous, I was just trying to earn enough to pay my bills

Nevertheless another asked if I ever got any sleep

The amount of my check was disclosed and it made them weep

To me if nothing is attempted nothing will be gained

I kept it together and tried not to go insane

I was clearly on a meticulous mission

Wanting to be the one to start the ignition

Patience

Marvel not, but I am patiently waiting for the Lord

What an honor to be finally with Him on one accord

On that day of trembling, when the trumpet sounds

When my mortal body will finally be heaven bound

In the twinkling of an eye transformed to immortality

When the angels and I will be having a splendid party

No chaotic schedules, courtroom drama or judges

No hiring, firing, infidelity or prolonged grudges

No more striving for possible perfection

Where human's destiny is simple rage and rejection

The sanctified Lord Jesus has never lost a case

That is why I will patiently wait, but at his own pace

Patterns

I see lovely patterns in my eyes

Some look round while others look geometric

Several of them make me unhappy and some make me eccentric

A number of them are extensive and others are quite narrow

Various ones make me feel like flying like a sparrow

Certain ones are beautifully designed and some are offbeat

Some make me energetic and others make me neat

Particular ones make shout, some make me smile

Some give me understanding, some make me see

All these patterns are just a beautiful extension of me

Perimeters

Established to keep you away from me

So I would have a chance to be totally free

They say absence makes the heart grow fonder

In this case I hope it drifts and just wander

When I can clearly establish some space

I will hope my absence you can embrace

Personalities

Personalities surround us all day long

A number of them are just plain wrong

One protects you from calamity and recognize

The other is quick to make you traumatized

One is loving, admiring, and never judges

The other splurges with gifts and won't hold grudges

One is unselfish and reasonably calm

Whichever fits you, there is no need to ring the alarm

They identify who we are as a spiritual being

That innermost personality remains to be seen

Pipe Dreams

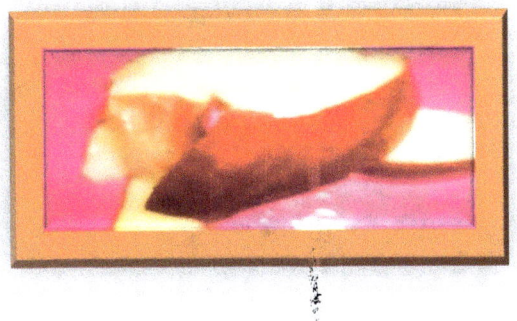

A mistress thought she ran our household

Doing things that were quite daring and bold

Right under our noses planning trips and going places

Only to leave her footprints and traces

All while the rest of the family was either at work, worship or play

Her schemes and trickeries has left her in dismay

Like the walls of Jericho, all things did fall and came to an end

She cannot turn back the hands of time or try to defend

She will just have to live on the memories she so desperately created

With an unfaithful spouse she might blame saying he initiated

As any story goes it takes two to tango and try to make things right

Now I'm laughing at a fool who put her life in a plight

Dream on mistress, the family will continue to pray for you

That all your schemes will crumble and your dreams will come true

Please stay away from my family's business and life

Stop dreaming that someday you will become his wife

Poems

I love the versatility of rhymes

They remind me of the past and present times

They are earnest therapy all the while

Conveying my innermost thoughts that make me smile

I adore the way verses incline and freely flow

Poetries that continually give me an expressive afterglow

Poker Face

It must have been difficult for you

To sustain the whole shebang and still remain so true

Prayers

Prayers will always change everything

It can turn your losses into tremendous wins

Pray at all times, all night and all day

Things will change, it won't stay that way

Pray, pray, pray without ceasing all day and night

The Lord Jesus will take your worries out of your sight

Preacher

Please do not call me a preacher

I am only studying to be a good teacher

To teach others what my noble teachers taught me

To educate myself and be all I can be

Please do not call me a preacher

Ironically my spiritual life is my best feature

Precise

It is quite natural you make me glow

But the answer is definitely no

I was positively trying hard to let it go

Only to let my emotional state flow

For you to know you will not use me for a show

Pretty Face

There is more to a person than a pretty face

The hands are hardworking yet still silky as lace

The brain solves every solution that will certainly not be erased

The legs can walk, run and ride to places at a steady pace

The other body parts can do whatever is exciting with no disgrace

They work collectively and are desired for grace

A pretty face is a savor the body has to embrace

Promises

Nothing went well for me today

Only wish I had done it an alternative way

Cannot turn back the hands of time

For now everything will have to work out just fine

At the end of the day, I did my very best

God promises that He will take care of the rest

Quiet Words

Quaky why don't you just hush

Unique but lower your voice and just shut up

Imagine a world without noise and zip it

Every time you worship just try to be silent

Time after time just practice being speechless

Quintessential Me

Quiet

Unique

Interesting

Nice

Timid

Entertaining

Serious

Sensual

Enjoyable

Nutty

Trusting

Inspiring

Admirable

Loving

Rachel's Sweet Sixteen

Hello my birthday princess today is your sweet sixteen

What a day you have filled with activities fit for a queen

Do not get carried away and try to dress alike a little figurine

Goodbye fifteen, now just chill in your favorite blouse and blue jean

I'll have breakfast ready for you: a bagel, cheese, and sardines

Enjoy this day, it's your year to prepare for fragrant seventeen

You've been a shining star from birth from all that I've seen

You'll have a new pair of sneakers and a beautiful dress in aquamarine

Not to mention gifts from your sisters; don't think there's a trampoline

Continue being an example of God or mom will have to intervene

Recently

I recently removed you from my heart

I placed you with all the heavenly dwellings

That is where you belong

To give my heart an ease

That way it will not hurt as much

Therefore you will be forever protected from any harm

Nevertheless always close to my soul

To me that is how perfect you are

Recovery

I would like to fully heal and recover

But the old wounds still hurt, that is what I discover

I remain quiet and relatively challenging to impress

Meanwhile, abuse is an issue I will always address

Nobody should be tainted or abused

Tricked or embarrassingly misused, should I say the rest?

I am going to confess that I was raped

Trapped in a dark room with nowhere to escape

Tied to a bed, the sounds of evil was all I heard

To think this would not have an impact is really absurd

So now you heard it from the victim's mouth

Not merely hearing it from someone else and having any doubt

Relaxation Section

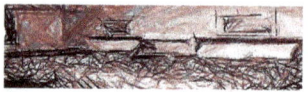

There are boundaries, so do not get the two mixed up
Undoubtedly work is not a place to get corrupt
Misidentifying a work zone for a relaxation section
Lusting and breaking rules just to get some affection
I know eight hours is more than you can handle
But do not alter it with undies and a burning candle
This is why you are in unnecessary suffering and expenses
Enticing a villain with mendacities and inessential pretenses
Seldom operative because of your extra work dealings
With the desperate charlatan that has no feelings
How do you identify that type as being sensual and great?
You come home still and eat out of your spouse's plate
You should have foreseen the dreadful warning sign
Of a dressed up muddle, thinking they are a fine design
That could not secure a partner to call their own
So they conceal, lust, undress, whimper and groan
Currently you are at the end of your tether, and busted
So finish your labor now since you could not be trusted
What can you show for the calories you dupes both burned?
Poor judgments, a guilty conscious and a partner's painful face
Of a secret affair, that gave birth at a respectful workplace

Repercussions

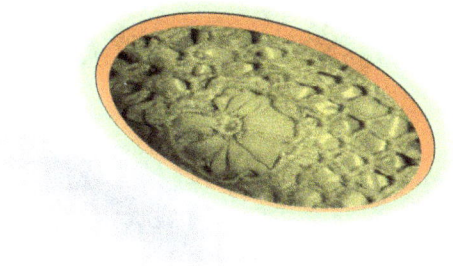

Be very aware of repercussions

It creeps up on you with sudden destruction

Never take what does not belong to you

In the end it will only make you very blue

You look at someone or something trying deceitfully to acquire it

With imminent consequence, will you endure it or be mentally fit

Just be mindful that what goes around comes around

Make sure that you are prepared to stand on solid ground

Robin Yawn

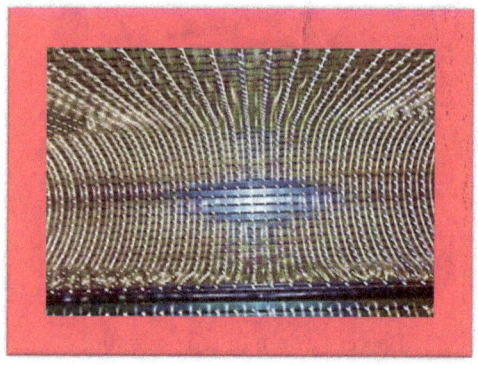

I know she was an angel sent from above

To brighten up everyone's lives like a little white dove

Pleasant, loyal, motivating and always caring

We will soon meet in heaven with all the God-fearing

We all love and truly miss you

Because your friendship and presence was forever true

Rest

When you have sufficient rest

The body functions at its best

Your mind becomes free, and your body has better mobility

Try to get adequate rest, this is a fact

Your overall health and wellness will have a great impact

Say What Is On Your Mind

Say what is on your mind

It may be sweetened or unkind

From the abundance of your heart the mouth starts speaking

Perhaps your words can send one laughing or weeping

Please reverberate it through your wall

It can liberate you or someone else and leave them standing tall

Rather to say what is on your mind

Than for you to conceal it and not let it unwind

Secret of Success

I learned the secret of success

It is pure devotion at its best

When you stumble and your back is against the wall

Get back up quickly; in the end you will be standing tall

Do not think of tripping again, or having a big fall

Your time is coming when you will be having a ball

Semester Blues

When the semester finally ended

I felt all my wounds were finally mended

I thought I was finally off the hook

Only to find out I misplaced my friend's book

Just to think of causing her pain

It is enough to drive me insane

Smile a While

Try hard to smile for a little while

Try, oh please try hard not to cry

For the Lord Jesus pledged He will be there

Just open up your heart and promise to care

His promises stay continually true

The decision is totally up to you

I know, I know my blessed Redeemer lives

So smile, smile, smile, for salvation is what He freely gives

Space

I need sufficient space to fashion my own atmosphere

I must get out of this untangled web of uncertainty

I will have to commit and secure a galaxy that is valid for my security

I'm to unclutter any baggage of improbability

So I can have enough space and imagination for creativity

I need space to construct and be part of this momentary human race

Spring Cleaning

Just an overall wholesome feeling

A time to rearrange and find spiritual healing

To liberate yourself of winter blues

Evenhandedly try gravitating to spring's good news

New drapes, mops, brooms, paint and fresh flowers

Hello spring cleaning, bring in the April showers

Stained Glass

It's difficult for me to envision

What lies beyond that colorful beauty?

What is hidden among those dominant colors?

What I can imagine is that if they are removed

Clarity will almost immediately become a reality

Standing Alone

The day finally came where I am standing alone

Zilch to relate to but pray and talk on the phone

Time has arisen for me to face reality

Life, and individuals change that is actuality

That dreams don't always come true

I could momentarily start making things new

By God's grace I will stay strong and strive

With everything in me as long as I am alive

Starry Night

Starry night does not hunger for any daylight

Seemingly they prefer night to do just what they like

A time for the cowardly, weary, wicked and the introverted

Thirsting for a starry night to hide or be converted

Not praying for the heated sunlight of the precious morning

Resting dreaming and hoping for afflictions to be released

A liberation and respite from their burdens to say the very least

Starry night all they all want from you is abundant peace

Stevens Forest Elementary School

With new renovations and an ultimate goal in mind
The staff and students model that success is what you'll find
Like what the positive behavioral intervention program will stress
To convey the message of PBIS learning and put it to the test
Being sincerely respectful, truthfully responsible and always ready
Working together to implement bully prevention is incredibly steady
Extracurricular activities and an integrated education are mentioned
Columbia, Maryland's pride without getting in contention
Now I am not emphasizing for your immediate registration
But in this community school a child's success is their only obligation
Former students will also let you know how the system works
Parent involvement and community support are just a few of the perks
I know the building was constructed in 1972
But your success here will have the world looking up to you
Preparation for middle school and high school is what they're coaching
A goal everyone here will keep fulfilling as the time is approaching

Stowaway

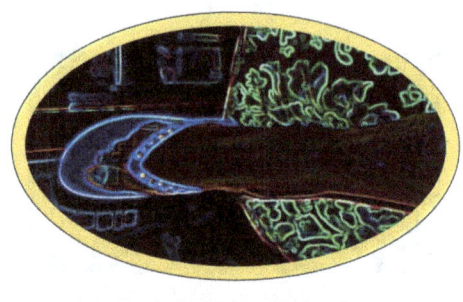

I was unceasingly treated like a stowaway

Abused and left to be thrown away

Shipwrecked and a fugitive that departed in dismay

Then the Almighty God sent His Angel my way

He saved me through the blood of Christ Jesus and taught me to pray

Now I am complete and content as I may

Nothing will keep me away from His love and that will always stay

His Holy Spirit will ensure that I never go astray

If I happen to stumble He promised to never treat me like a stowaway

He will remind me that I was purified by the blood of Christ anyway

And prompt me to hold steadfast and pray everyday

Stranger

You are to be loved and catered to at your request

Not treated like an alien but an honored guest

Given unconditional love like every human being

Not neglected like a tourist but someone always seen

Compassion and kindness is all you should see

An unfamiliar person is not what you will ever be

Surrender

Surrender your heart and life to the one and only Almighty God

Confess your sins to Jesus Christ to alleviate all pain and sorrow

You will certainly have a brighter day and a better tomorrow

To be with the Lord forever and walk the streets of pure gold

God Almighty has made you that promise that has long been foretold

Tameka

Preserving scripted revelations is her effortless mission

Pressing on without fear or hesitations is her true vision

Interpreting life as a carefree, discarding clueless emotions

Classifying them raw, intriguing and with realistic devotions

Do not underestimate her infinite strength and ability

She will inculcate in us her work with honesty and credibility

Or judge her immeasurable wisdom or insightful mindset

Her loyalty and kindness are the traits you will never forget

She continues to conquer all misfortunes as they entail

Like a conductor assuring passengers her train will never derail

Teacher

You motivate, inspire, monitor and set the tone

To educate everyone so they will never feel alone

You model, operate, provide and maintain

A true sense of value without having anything to gain

You supervise, finance, organize, and communicate

A code of ethical conduct that everyone can imitate

You are the rock of ages, through all the developmental stages

Be a true educator as long as you may

Continue to teach the something that nobody will ever take away

The Blue Ocean

I love to look at the blue ocean

Just to see the waves in slow motion

I get a glimpse of the different species of fish

But diving to the bottom is my only wish

To see the sedimentary rocks and seaweeds

The natural salt and the ocean breeze

I am dreaming of swimming to glory, can't you see

Yes, in the blue ocean is where you will find me

The Colors of My Emotions

My emotions occasionally are cloudy blue

When I am alone and do not hear from you

Infrequently it turns to apple red

If I do not convey what is being said

Perpetually it modifies to melon green

When someone is fixating on being very mean

Ostensibly it adjusts to tulip pink

When I sit alone and have some time to think

Permanently it transforms to stone grey

When I can envision true love is here to stay

Continuously it changes to banana yellow

Just visiting someone to say a quick hello

Infrequently it will turn to chocolate brown

If I can image affection will always be around

A synopsis of all my emotions is primarily black

That is when they are utterly on the right track

The Good Book

The Holy Bible to me is the only good book

I will lament on it and take a closer look

It will give me wisdom and set me free

But the decision of salvation is completely up to me

So in the meantime I will continue to surrender

Committing to the words of this book is my main agenda

The Month of April

The month of April inspired me

To resume writing and be all I can be

Books, pens, markers, tablet and pencils

My memory unfolded like a design from a stencil

Beautiful colors of all the exotic flowers

All in the month of April showers

I even wrote a sermonette I had to preach

Satisfied souls I'm sure I was able to reach

The Seventh Day

The Seventh day is the Sabbath of the Lord Almighty God

He created it as the day of rest after he created the heavens and earth

After that He created us from the dust of the ground

Before then the animals and nature were around

Almighty God sanctified and blessed the seventh day

A time to rest, worship and refrain from work and play

The Wife and A Mistress

A devoted wife is longsuffering and has a lot to gain

A mistress disappears in times of trouble trying hard to remain sane

A virtuous wife is content and free of guilt

A mistress has to hide and run for shade under huge a quilt

A devoted wife is precious and lives her lifetime fulfilling her dream

That a mistress tries to imitate by sneaking only to make her scream

A mistress needs to learn what God puts together no man can take away

Try to learn this valuable lesson mistress and do not let it go astray

Attempt to be fully clad at work and play to stay on an accurate track

Then maybe I would not be tempted to stage an attack

Meanwhile mistress try to think of the stolen memories you created

Ponder the story of how an unfaithful spouse is dismal and overrated

Daydream mistress until you see you got zilch from doing wrong

By the grace of God I am the wife that shines and remains strong

Three Words

The only three words I know for sure

Is that I love you, and that there is no cure

I love you, yes I truly love you

I love you; I love you, so much is true

I indeed love you forevermore

Only you will I unrelentingly love and adore

Tickle Me

Tickle me and make me giggle

Just enough to make me wiggle

Play me a sentimental song

With a song, wiggle and giggle, who can go wrong?

Time Management

Try to run your business on your own time

A suitable time you can call your own and is fine

Without being bullied by overhead bosses

That will soon make you think about sudden losses

Always give yourself some respectful space

Challenge yourself without feeling like you're competing in a race

Are you trying to get to the mountain top?

The pressure will only make you stop

In the end it is still your own time

It's not costing anyone else a single dime

Timothy Belton

Working on his ultimate goal to march upward to Zion

Timothy Belton has the strength of a ferocious lion

He is one of our church's greatest spiritual motivators

As much as we need directions with a navigator

He has the heart of a resilient flying hawk

That is his vision in another life so he can fly and talk

In his quiet times he likes to meditate

A routine everyone can easily imitate

Subsequently he likes to take nature walks

Where he and Christ Jesus have countless talks

He is very devoted to his family and loves to exercise

With those in mind he will not compromise

His daily passion is to spread the gospel of Jesus Christ our Lord

Where one day all saints will gather with one accord

Be blessed, strong and courageous and pull through for us all

With the love of Christ and family, you will never fall

To Be

To be needed is a special feeling of love

It's like receiving a pure blessing from God above

To be appreciated is to be honored and cherished

Not feeling like being shipwrecked and many perished

To be blessed is worth more than the abundance of the rich

For who God blesses no man curses that is plain without any glitch

Torrid Tales

Echoes of my childhood days

A bright and blistering future

Shining through the sun's rays

Unbearable

It was all good until you hanged up the phone

That triggered a bit of anger right down to my bone

It is okay to be friends with my significant other

Just as long as it is respectful, then I will unquestionably not bother

The calls and texting became exceedingly out of control

Emotions and indignation started taking a toll

What were you trying to find?

I am not trying to be unkind

But there is nothing to find until you find yourself

Until then you can dispense your burdens and gain some respect

Unfaithful

It is a shame someone had to eventually die
Trying to help me figure out the question why
Why do women sometimes act like hoes?
Wanting everyone that comes and goes
Flip the script, what if your foot was in someone's shoes?
Will it fit? Or do you even have any of the clues
What if your significant other did that to you?
Would you leave him and say he was not true?
So quit messing around and making others blue
Every house was built on a strong foundation
What legacy will you leave for your generation?
Being unfaithful is such a disgrace
All it does is generate pain and shatters the human race
You will identify when karma comes around
It won't be long before your name is all around town

Unique Monique

My first born and a very beautiful African Queen

She is everything to me and in the very least not at all mean

There is nobody that understands her and loves her better

Besides Almighty God, mom's love is like a friendship letter

She overcomes everything without being fearful

Shedding tears quietly so you will always see her cheerful

Even her very existence may be a subject of controversy

But she ensures you that her plan is to overcome all adversity

A beautiful mom who tries her best to survive daily

Ignoring harsh words from critics and doing her best to impel

That God is the only judge and that is why she will always excel

Unpredictable

Just meditated and objectively changed my mind

I did not mean to be so unkind

I just cancelled our planned extravagant vacation

I needed privacy from the work station

When there is sufficient discretion and space

Then being unpredictable will exhibit no trace

Validation

It happened suddenly one day

Things unsurprisingly went my way

My hands reached out and touched the sky

The day you all of a sudden smiled and simply said hi

That is when my lonely heart was set free

The day you decided to finally notice me

Not that I needed any justification

But that word liberated me with abundant clarification

Just one word permitted me to stretch and touch the sky

Now satisfied and out of the captivity I tried so long to untie

Valuable Lesson

Early in the morning after a relaxing time walking

I decided I should learn to listen more and do less talking

If I need something I dare not beg or borrow

It may lead me to acquire a heap of sorrow

I will now look, glance and stare

But I will not plead, no I will not dare

I may recognize that what I anticipate might need some revision

Only to discover it was far more than what I had envisioned

So next time I do not have I will certainly learn to do without

Even if I have to bellow, whimper or pout

Through my experience I established why curiosity killed the cat

Because unless he is lucky nothing or nobody will ever bring him back

Vanished

You erased ten years of my mind

Even though you were not trying to be unkind

A decade of empty memories is what is left

I am not sure if it was intentional or cyber theft

Not a piece of document could be traced

That is the day when my computer memory got erased

Visualize

How wide is the word wide?

I will leave it for you to decide

Is it just a word with four letters?

Or do we use it as a mere go-getter?

How wide is the word wide?

I think that question will expand your mind

Maybe then your thoughts can unwind

Three inches, two feet, rectangular, or whatever you see

Your wide is certainly too narrow to see

Volunteer

Please take a little time to volunteer

It is the best way to show somebody you truly care

You will make a difference and brighten someone's day

From babies, toddlers, teens to adults if you may

Don't ever think about not getting paid

God has sacrificed His Son Christ Jesus so you can have it made

Waiting for Misty Morning

Just sitting waiting for misty morning to come

Neutrally waiting to peek at the rising of the blazing sun

To jump start praying, organizing, doing errands and be on the run

Waiting for the colorful rays of the sunset's shadows and reflections

To always tell someone they are loved and created from perfection

Anxiously awaiting hearing birds and to converse with people in sight

I know then that God granted me another day of His marvelous light

Water

Simply known as the greatest nutrient

It's also the body's best survival instrument

A source for everything needed for living

Building, planting, nutrition and gift giving

Although it plays a role of damaging and comfort

It creates magic at amusement parks and resorts

Raining from the heavens splash, splash

Or just bottling it for some cold cash

A pure gift the sea animals can testify

God's gift to mankind that we need not justify

What Is It Like to be Dead?

Initializing, no rent, or mortgages to pay

No emotionally distressed person calling another one gay

No deceptive friends, jealously, betrayals or utility bills

No greed, inexpensive and luxurious clothing or tricky wills

The relief of headaches, sickness and pain

Who are we kidding, the dead know nothing and have zilch to gain

Once there is life there is hope you will see

We are alive now, therefore we are free

Live one day at a time, bear good times and hardship, and do not bend

In the meantime be patient and endure to the very end

When

When, is the word of the essence

When will I do this? When will I do that?

Once I get here, when will I get there?

What time will be of interpretation?

While I wait for this, should I do that?

After I complete this task, what should I do next?

The minute I get nearby, what will be my next move?

As soon as I prepare for something, would I include this?

If I dwell on a thought, will I accomplish it?

Time waits for no man, the time of when is at this moment

The embodiment of my character depends on when

When I do anything is up to me, but the time should be the present

The most important thing is to do all for our God in heaven

Withered

Seems facetious that you have allowed yourself to gradually decline

Just because you refused to change your conduct and be refined

It was not enough that we are all bearing your pain

Certain things just need modifications in order for you to abstain

A turnaround can be a lesson when you practice with the right tool

But instead you continue to be fruitless and play the fool

The leaves plummet and wither from the tree of your crumbled mind

If it is God's will when you awake your loved ones are all you will find

Yesterday

You ask where is beautiful yesterday

Where the ocean breeze made the oak trees sway

When our hair was very long and thick

We frequently felt like performing in a disco flick

Well forget yesterday, here is today

Live it one minute at a time until you go away

You Can

You can travel anywhere without fear

You can talk to anyone just make it clear

You can do anything with God's permission

When they aim at you with a bow and arrow

Remind them that God made you His mighty sparrow

Zeal

Beyond expressive comprehension is the way you make me feel

Senseless and passionate but I know when my emotions are really real

More eagerness than getting a buzzer beater on a basketball court

More enthusiasm than billions of dollars to own the teams of that sport

Extreme passion is felt watching you pass by with a feeling of glee

A fiery desire to always be where you are in your fancy gear with me

Blissfully I lose my ability to process anything within range of you

Nothing will ever change or appease this overzealous feeling for you

Zing Zap Fair

It is the annual Zing Zap Fair, can you solve this puzzle?

Will you jump up and down while trying to juggle?

Laugh out loud when you miss the lane and trip and fall

Throw around these colored sponge balls big and small

Toss the Frisbees in the hollow bucket in the sand

Throw the darts at the water balls to pop them but watch your hand

Spray the water gun to make the rubber ducky run but guard your eyes

Blow some bubbles and see them elevate to the sky

The Zing Zap Fair will bring out the kid in you

Leave all your worries behind and try a Ferris wheel ride or two

Pop balloons to win a large teddy bear that is a big prize

Oh look that is me in the clown dress heavily disguised

Over there you will find Oreos, corn dogs, lemonade, and cheese fries

I'm happy I finally won the large teddy bear after many tries

About the Poet

 Wynette McKenzie started writing poetry when she was eight years old. Her poetry is inspired by her childhood and motherhood. She is a certified Early Childhood Educator and continues to draw inspiration from her life as a Christian and her work with children.

www.ingramcontent.com/pod-product-compliance
Lightning Source LLC
Chambersburg PA
CBHW062141280426
43673CB00072B/100